A New Guide
to Becoming One
with
Parama Shiva

A Spiritual Feast
of New Freedoms:

Infinite Bliss Now

Other Books
by Ramanananda Maharshi

1. ATMA DARSHANA ANUBHUTI [Experience of Darshan of Parama Shiva or Parama Atma] – In Telugu
2. SHAKTHIPATHAM - In Telugu, Hindi
3. The Secret of Shirdi Sai's Benevolence – In Telugu, English, Hindi, Marathi, Tamil
4. The Secret of Service to Shirdi Sai – In Telugu, English
5. Divine Love Songs on Shirdi Sai – In Telugu
6. The Hidden Secrets behind Guru Disciple Relationship – In Telugu, Tamil
7. Shirdi Sai Anugraha Seva Rahasyam – In Telugu, English, Hindi
8. The Divine Life History of Siddha Yogini RadhaKrishna Mayi – In Telugu, Hindi.

After meeting the families of 27 direct disciples of Shirdi Sai, interviewing their children, grandchildren and great grandchildren, Maharshi wrote 27 books describing their connection with Shirdi Sai, such as how Baba guided them, how their later generations are benefiting from an ancestor-connection with such a great Parama Guru like Shirdi Sai.

Books in Telugu.

1. Life history of Mahalsapathi.
2. Life history of Shyama.
3. Life history of Taatya.
4. Life history of Nana Chandorkar.
5. Life history of Kaka Saheb Dixit.
6. Life history of Pradhan.
7. Life history of Smt. Pradhan.

8. Life history of Abdul Baba.
9. Life history of Hemadpant.
10. Life history of Tatya Saheb Noolkar.
11. Life history of Nimonkar.
12. Life history of Sapathnekar.
13. Life history of Damodar Rasane.
14. Life history of Kushalchand.
15. Life history of Khaparde.
16. Life history of Smt. Khaparde.
17. Life history of Chandrabai Borkar.
18. Life history of Dhoomal.
19. Life history of Purandhare.
20. Life history of Laxmibai Shinde.
21. Life history of Tarabai.
22. Life history of Smt. Tarkhad.
23. Life history of Adakar.
24. Life history of Nana Saheb Dengle.
25. Life history of Bayyaji Appaji Patil.
26. Life history of Gavankar.
27. Life history of Mirikar.

Books on Shiva or Vedas

1. The Shiva God of Gods-AdiGuru-
   ParamaPurusha – In Telugu, English, Hindi
2. Purusha Suktam – In Telugu

A NEW GUIDE
TO BECOMING ONE
WITH
PARAMA SHIVA

A SPIRITUAL FEAST
OF NEW FREEDOMS:

INFINITE BLISS NOW

Ramanananda
Maharshi

A New Guide to Becoming One
with Parama Shiva
by Ramanananda Maharshi

ISBN: 978-1-947477-00-1
© Copyright 2017 All Rights Reserved
First printed English edition 2017
Publishers: Shirdi Sai Anugraha Peetam.

Contact Information:
    Phone:
        India: 951-597-6923
        USA: 978-996-4708
Email: meditationswithmaharshi@gmail.com
Website: https://www.ramananandamaharshi.com/

Cover graphics by Manoj Vijayan
Translation by Chandra Velpula
Editing by Margra Muirhead, Ginny Porter, and
    Chandra Velpula

Dedication

It is with a heart full of love and infinite
gratitude that I dedicate this book to
Parama Shiva,
who has so richly given me of his Love,
Self-realization and a divine opportunity
to share his true teachings with the world.

Contents

Notes to the Reader

The immense flow of divine SPIRIT pouring thru Ramanananda Maharshi's teachings begins to free devotees, and will ultimately release them from the confines of restrictive rules based on thousands of years of ancient rituals and beliefs. This new freedom will open their hearts to behold the formless and to experience the Oneness connecting all Life.

The powerful message of Divine Love that continually pours through Maharshi's teachings will touch every aspect of your life with new and positive energies. Any sincere seekers who commit to adopting this new way of daily meditations will find their lives are changed forever.

Maharshi gives his answers below to devotees' questions that will provide readers with a sense of his enormous commitment to assisting seekers in reaching an enlightened state. His answers also reveal the importance of this book as a guide for those who may be newcomers to this path—and also as providing opportunities for anyone who is drawn in deeper to make a dedicated study of his teachings. The necessity of making a personal commitment to daily meditation is also explained.

1. What has been given you from Shiva as your primary teaching goal for this lifetime?

Answer

The way Maharshi explains it is that Shiva is primarily directing Maharshi to share a higher knowledge of Truth. He is now receiving increased vibrations to share more knowledge of Truth teachings with the seekers...Only a Self-realized Guru can explain Truth and instill this knowledge in a seeker's heart.

2. Would you share your inner directive for the 18 Day Silent Meditations and for this book?

Answer

In the summer of 2016, many misunderstandings were being spread about due to wrong things being discussed about who Shirdi Sai Baba is. When this disturbed Maharshi's mind he decided Silent meditations would be the best means to rectify these errors. Actually, it has been a meditative state that drew Maharshi to sit in Silence just like a hungry person gets drawn into a restaurant to eat food.

When Maharshi sits in meditation, divine teachings of Truth keep flowing out just like water keeps coming out in the sand next to the sea. During the 18 day deeksha, this divine flow of higher teachings was formulated into the meditation messages that now comprise this book.

3. What did you observe from the devotees' comments about their experiences?

Answer

To be frank, each individual devotee's experience would speak for itself. Devotees experience the most, just as when they go near a jasmine flower, they would experience its fragrance, but jasmine does not know its own fragrance ... those who come and meditate in my presence or meditate remotely during meditation sessions are the ones who receive my tapo shakthi (vibration) and experience the fragrance of Soul according to the depth of their spiritual journey. As they receive the flow of Divine energy they will experience much more in meditation than they do from just seeing my human form.

4. Who would be most ideally prepared to benefit from this book? What would be the future benefits for individuals who will continue to study this book??

Answer

Seekers who are really heart hungry with an intense longing for Infinite Bliss will begin to experience Infinite Bliss while continuing their studies of this book if they begin to understand and follow the guidance that is given.

For sincere seekers who want to eliminate unhappiness, sadness, these will be eliminated.

Those who have questions about the Divine Presence and whether It exists or not will become increasingly confident, through their individual experiences, that the Divine does exist.

They will receive inner inspiration and motivation to meditate. As they read and seek to understand these teachings more thoroughly, their minds are being purified and prepared to receive divine thoughts from "On High."

5. Does this book provide a sufficient explanation of principles for beginning students to use as a foundation to meditate upon?

Answer

For beginning students, this path is like a royal road…It is easy for the person who may not know the Shastras or Vedas, because he or she needs only to trust the principles and teachings within this book and follow the "right road."

6. Are there any different benefits to be derived from reading the book followed by regular meditations in these three ways?

   1. Sitting in Maharshi's presence in person
   2. Joining Maharshi remotely for online meditations

3. Meditation at home with no image of Maharshi

Would each option provide a differing degree of preparation for progressing on the spiritual path?

Answer

The first one is like sitting by the sea and enjoying directly what it is being offered.

The second one is like watching the sea on a TV— they still enjoy the bliss, but less than the one sitting next to the sea.

The third one is like climbing the stairs—one step at a time, slowly.

7. While continuing to study this book, what would be the most important pursuits for students wishing to enhance their journey on the spiritual path if they are unable to be in the presence of a Living Siddha Guru?

Answer

Commitment to daily meditation is needed and putting these principles into practice will be essential in each individual's daily life and circumstance.

Divine Grace provides that when it is not possible to be in the presence of a Living Siddha Guru, any pure hearted one who reaches out to him can still touch the hem of his undivided garment and receive blessings.

In addition, participation with other devotees for a satsang or meditation would also be very helpful.

Maharshi explains how it would be valuable for a person to reach out to him or call upon him silently anytime—when meditating, studying, participating in a group or facing a challenge, because a Maharshi is aware of all those who make a sincere request for his help. It is his mission and joy to call forth all seekers to New Freedom and to welcome them to a Spiritual Feast of Infinite Bliss Now.

Rules for Deeksha Meditation

1. This period is dedicated to silence (mounam), meditation, and reading.

2. Everyone can participate in this deeksha.

3. The deeksha begins on 8 Aug 2016 at 9 AM by chanting OM 3 times.

4. Participants should not perform any kind of external worship of any form of god or guru. For seekers who worship the Soul, there is no need for external worship.

5. Participants should not light external lamps (diya). Seekers who light a lamp to the Soul do not need any external lamps. Those who don't want to participate in this deeksha can light the external lamps.

6. Participants should not read any shastras or god/goddess related books or even Self-realized masters' books. They should only read books related to the Soul [Atma Tattva].

7. If possible, meditate in the presence of Maharshi.

8. If a participant can't meditate in the direct presence of Maharshi, one should meditate during the same time of the session at their homes. This way they will receive the divine vibration and potency from Maharshi.

9. Participants should meditate 4 hours every day during the scheduled times below (Indian Std. Time):

> First Session: 9:30 AM–10:30 AM
> Second Session: 11:30 AM–12:30 PM
> Third Session: 5:00 PM–6:00 PM
> Fourth Session: 6:30 PM–7:30 PM

10. Participants should not eat meat.

11. Participants should maintain celibacy during this period.

12. Ladies can do this deeksha during their periods and also even if there is a death or new born in the house. Just as Parama Atma is beyond all this, this Siddha deeksha is also beyond all this.

13. Participants should chant only on the formless Shiva's name or OM; they should not chant any form of a god's or a guru's name.

14. Participants should stop the meditations on any form of god/goddess or guru and should focus on the formless oneness Shiva.

15. Participants should not visit any temples, should not take dips/baths in holy teerthams or rivers. Seekers will be taking a dip in the streams of their Soul, and there is no need of external temples or holy teerthams or rivers.

16. There is no need to bathe the head in the morning and evening. Seekers who are receiving a bath for the Soul do not need any special baths for the physical body.

17. Participants should not sit with seekers who are doing external worships or people in the worldly life. They should not touch them. They should not listen to their words.

18. Participants with kundalini moments should take precautions and control measures to find a balance and sit quietly. If they lose control, deeksha is not fulfilled.

19. Those who can't participate all 18 days, can try for 1 or 3 or 5 or 9 or 11 days.

20. Sitting and meditating in the presence of Maharshi is much, much greater than meditating at home. During this deeksha

period, meditation in the presence of Maharshi is even more powerful.

21. Deeksha will end on 26 August 2016 morning at 10AM by chanting OM 3 times.

1st Day

Just Do Meditation

To meditate is the best and most wonderful way to worship God. Mind will never be in your control through any external or mental forms of worship you performed inside the mind. To give some work to the mind is to move away from God. So don't do any work inside the mind. Just do meditations, and then the mind will be in your control. You will be establishing perfection in the worship of the Soul.

2nd Day

Experiencing Infinite Bliss

Most people think of God as having form, but any form is just an illusion and not the truth. God is formless as the most wondrous flow of infinite bliss. It is not easy for everyone to enjoy this bliss. Only those with a one-pointed focus of the mind can experience this divine flow when they quiet their mind and enter their heart's cave. When the seeker experiences the divine flow of infinite bliss the individual's soul, mind, and intellect become purified and energized. .

Many people know that God is the treasure of all knowledge; however, only Siddha Yogis know that God is the source of this entire treasure that flows as infinite bliss. One cannot receive the wisdom of great intelligence and awareness of higher knowledge by just reading the shastras. This will only occur when one receives the darshan of the magnificent divine light glowing inside the heart. So drop the external worship and make the mind quiet without its turning outward. Then you will experience the flow of infinite bliss, and also have the darshan of wonderfully glowing divine light in the heart.

3rd Day

"I am the jiva" to "I am Brahman"

There exists a strong "I am the jiva" feeling that rises up in everyone like a Mount Meru. It is not easy to wipe out this feeling completely in one try. First, with an unwavering commitment to meditations (Dhyana Tapasu), one has to lessen the jiva feelings. These will vanish in proportion to the seeker's increasing discovery of the divine knowledge—"I am Brahman."

Only when jivatma becomes one with the Parama Atma, will the stronger feelings of divine knowledge that "I am Brahman" become an enduring conviction within. Meditation acts as a wonderful "medicine" to wipe out the jivatma. Only when gold is burnt in the fire (Agni) will its purity shine, and only when jivatma is burnt in the "fire of meditation" will it shine as pure atma. The more you meditate, the more jivatma becomes purified.

A pure individual soul can't continue in the worldly ways of maya—as the purified soul will no longer turn outward.

After the individual soul experiences the bliss with Parama Atma, it naturally drops worldly happiness and continually seeks to enjoy the bliss with Parama Atma.

The individual soul, who previously could not live without maya, now because of meditations, craves for a divine state and can't live without Parama Atma even for one moment. One who attains this divine state is called Jivanmukta or Avadhuta. So make every effort to achieve this state.

4th Day

Bath to the Individual Soul (Atma Snanam)

Water from a river or a sea can only cleanse the impurities present on the physical body. This water doesn't have the strength to cleanse the impurities of the mind or give the wealth of pious qualities (suguna sampatti). Those who meditate to bathe in the flow of the infinite bliss (Brahmananda) can cleanse the impurities of the mind and they acquire a wealth of pious qualities (suguna sampatti). To experience this divine bath to the soul (Atma snanam) strengthens the soul (Atma balam) and blesses human beings with a magnetic Brahmic aura (Brahmavarchas), and with a spiritual halo (Brahma-tejas).

Those devoted to meditations are the fortunate ones that can take a dip in the streams of the atma, and receive a bath to the soul (Atma snanam). Streams of infinite bliss only flow in the hearts of pious beings that do the meditations. When the streams of infinite bliss flow during the meditations, the seeker receives an inner cleansing just as a soiled cloth is cleansed when it is washed. All accumulations from bad deeds (papa malam) and faults in the subconscious mind (chitta doshalu) are completely eliminated; therefore, seekers will get the Darshan of the Parama Atma by being established in a pure and quiet mind with an unsurpassed intellect.

The result from being established in a quiet mind in dhyana samadhi for even a moment is equivalent to dipping into one crore (1,000,000) holy streams (teethams). The grandeur of a meditation such as this is extraordinary.

So as we practice meditations with great dedication, determination, intensity, and patience streams of infinite bliss should flow through the seeker's inner space—and then the seeker will become Brahma Gnani by being completely freed from the results of all previous bad deeds and all attachments.

5th Day

Real Maha Lakshmi

In this world, many people are very well aware of goddess Lakshmi but not many know who Maha Lakshmi is. Maha Shakti (Primal Energy) which is embedded inside the individual soul is called Maha Lakshmi; she is also called Kundalini Shakti, Parabrahmani, and Parameswari.

While goddess Lakshmi blesses with a rain of money, Maha Lakshmi blesses with a downpour of infinite bliss. While a snake is hidden inside a mud hill (pamu putta), Maha Lakshmi is hidden in the inner self of every being. As a snake is awakened with the sound of a nadaswaram, and Maha Lakshmi is awakened from within the individual soul when a seeker does meditations. Once Maha Lakshmi is awakened, infinite bliss will slowly begin flowing. As their awakening becomes stronger and deeper, the seeker experiences a simultaneous increase in the flow of infinite bliss.

Just as the water from the river Ganges flows with force downward, Maha Lakshmi flows with force upward toward Parama Atma. Just as the Ganges pulls along many things as it flows down, so is Maha Lakshmi flowing upward, pulling mind, intellect and the individual soul with it. As the river flows down and becomes one with the sea, Maha Lakshmi flows up and becomes one with Parama Shiva. Along with Maha Lakshmi, mind, intellect and the individual soul also merge with Parama Shiva. This merging is called Self-realization or the union of the jiva and Brahman.

When Maha Lakshmi becomes
one with Parama Shiva,
the entire human being is purified—
divine energy fills every cell
and every atom of the body.

When the goddess is worshiped during the month of Shravan, human beings are blessed only with wealth, but when we worship Maha Lakshmi, we receive along with wealth, many divine powers, worldly and divine fortune and liberation.

To meditate is real worship to Maha Lakshmi.
To meditate is real prayer to Maha Lakshmi.
To meditate is real devotion to Maha Lakshmi.

So do meditations with dedication and one-pointed focus to enjoy the ultimate blessings of true infinite bliss from Maha Lakshmi.

Pamu putta: mud hill in which a snake lives

Lakshmi: Hindu goddess of wealth, fortune and prosperity

Nadaswaram: Musical instrument to which a snake dances.

Parameswari: She who is the ultimate goddess

Ganges: Ganges River, Great River of the plains of the northern Indian subcontinent.

6th Day

Anger, Lust, Bad Qualities and Attachments

Even when the gurus or shastras order them to quit, human beings can't easily relinquish anger, lust, bad qualities (gunas) and attachment to happiness from worldly things. Although human beings may have the wisdom to promise themselves to get rid of these qualities, it is still very difficult to accomplish this. Even by reading shastras or strotras, doing poojas, worshipping gods or goddesses, or dipping into holy streams (Teerthams), human beings can't eliminate them completely.

Anger, lust, bad qualities and attachments to the worldly happiness will begin to decrease from the moment infinite bliss starts to flow within the inner soul, mind and intellect. This great change happens only when a seeker devotes himself to deeper meditations each day. Human discussions and external practices have no benefit for the seeker; only silent meditation gives the highest benefit. Meditation is the best sadhana to cleanse or purify the individual soul (jivatma). Maha Shakti awakens for those beings whose soul has been significantly strengthened. When the seekers are established in the awakening of the Maha Shakti, they will then be established in Oneness of the jiva and Brahman.

The reason the individual soul strength is weak is because lust, anger, bad qualities (gunas), and attachments to happiness from worldly things still continue to linger in the seeker. Only with deeper meditations when the seeker experiences the flow of infinite bliss, does the strength of the soul increase and all the faults or imperfections are eliminated completely.

So say good-bye to all the unnecessary talk; drop sushka (essenceless or empty) Vedanta, and quit your reliance on external forms of worship. Always immerse yourself in deep meditations and then you will become true Brahma Gnani and experience the infinite bliss.

7th Day

Living Siddha Guru and Darshan of Parama Shiva

Parama Shiva exists everywhere in this world. He is omnipresent in every atom, every cell of the human body, every plant, every animal— everywhere. One cannot have the Darshan of Parama Shiva by seeing through the physical eyes. The only place one can have the crystal clear Darshan of Parama Shiva is in the inner sanctum of one's own heart. Through meditation when you enter into the inner sanctum of your heart—only then will you get the Darshan of Parama Shiva.

Parama Shiva is the home for all divine powers and siddhis. When a deep inner connection is established through dedicated meditations— then divine powers and siddhis naturally flow to you as a seeker. It is not only these that flow; you will also acquire divine characteristics and pious qualities of Parama Shiva.

This great opportunity of establishing a connection with Parama Shiva never comes easily to the seekers. Each seeker must be conscientious in devoting ample time to meditation and be wholehearted in one's worship. During this process of meditations and worship individual seekers need to drop their worldly enjoyments and do this practice with a quiet mind. Another option for the seeker is to selflessly serve a living Siddha Guru and do meditations in his presence.

Worshipping statues of gods in the temples or statues of Masters that attained mahasamadhi is much different than worshiping with a living Siddha Guru. Being in a living Siddha Guru's presence is much more powerful and attaining this privilege does not come easily. Just as one instantly smells the perfume once inside a perfume shop, a spiritual seeker will experience the flow of infinite bliss as soon as he/she enters the presence of a living Siddha Guru. Very easily and without any effort, the seeker's soul enters into their heart.

Everyone in this world, including illiterates, learned persons, spiritual seekers, sanyasis, or householders, can only have the Darshan of Parama Shiva either by the divine touch of a living Siddha Guru or by the grace of a living Siddha Guru.

In this the current Kaliyuga or Yuga, which is covered with impurities, it is not possible for everyone to do meditations consistently and to keep the mind calm, quiet and pure. Only very rarely can individuals achieve this all alone. That is why one needs to approach a living Siddha Guru and serve him; however, service alone is not enough. You have to meditate in the presence of a living Siddha Guru. Then and only then will one have Darshan of Parama Shiva.

8ᵗʰ Day

Mind Longing for Infinite Bliss

Mind is a reflection of maya. In the beginning the seeker's mind naturally runs toward maya in its pursuit of worldly happiness—just as a young child naturally runs after his mother for his every need. Through our meditations, we have to make this "running" mind begin to experience the flow of infinite bliss. Then instead of running toward worldly happiness, the mind will turn inward and run toward Parama Atma inside. When the mind experiences infinite bliss, then it will quickly lose its naturally jumpy nature.

Meditation will also start to dissolve the vasanas inside the mind. Because of this, the mind not only loses its desires related to worldly happiness, but also has a deep aversion toward worldly desires. Without any desires for worldly happiness, the mind will always have a great longing for infinite bliss with Shiva (Paramananadam). So we have to meditate and make sure the mind is always turned inward to merge with the ocean of infinite bliss with Shiva.

Mind and prana are like two closely paired thieves. These two can act as deceivers to make the individual soul (jivatma) suffer in the worldly life, and they can also give orders for the individual soul to feel worldly happiness inside. Prana always stimulates (or triggers) the mind, and the mind in-turn, always stimulates (or triggers) the individual soul. In order for the individual soul to become one with the Parama Atma, first, we must first cleanse the mind of its naturally worldly ways. We do this through meditations until the mind is completely immersed in the infinite bliss of Shiva.

At this point the mind will stop harassing the individual soul and be quiet. In that very moment when the mind becomes quiet, the individual soul will merge with and shine like the Parama Atma.

The quiet mind can also become jumpy because of the movement in the prana. When the prana is jumpy, the mind may also get becomes jumpy. When the mind loses its quietness, then the vasanas and samskaras inside the mind rise up. When vasanas and samskaras rise up, the mind loses its happiness and will forget the infinite bliss with Shiva and return to the desires for worldly happiness. This cycle continues until all the vasanas and samskaras are completely dissolved.

Therefore we have to continually do meditations with our utmost devotion and dedication to control the prana and the mind so that the individual soul will merge with the Parama Atma. Then the seeker will become pure Brahma Gnani, and be totally free from the grip of maya.

9th Day

The Aura of Living Siddha Guru

One does not have to pray to the Fire [Agni], "Please grant me warmness." One can experience the warmness just by sitting in the presence of the Fire. One does not have to ask the jasmine flower, "Please spread the fragrance." One experiences the fragrance by simply being in the presence of the jasmine flower. Also like this, we do not have to pray to a living Siddha Guru, "Please grant me the Yoga Shakti." By our simply sitting in the presence of a living Siddha Guru, without any request, we can receive the flow of Yoga Shakti with full force.

The aura of a living Siddha Guru is enormous and high-powered when compared to the aura of people who are not on a spiritual path, or to seekers worshipping various gods, or to gurus who are not self-realized.

Seekers will be immersed in the aura of a living Siddha Guru if they are in the Guru's presence, whether meditating or not. When the seeker is blessed with such an opportunity, their subtle body becomes energized. Their mind becomes filled with divine energy and becomes quiet. Their individual soul (jivatma) will be bathed and their impurities cleansed in a divine bath by being completely filled with the flow of Yoga Shakti. This bath is also called a "divine bath to the Atma." Seekers should always remember that meditating in the presence of a living Siddha Guru is a bath to the Atma and choose every opportunity for this to occur.

The aura of a guru who is not self-realized is like a darkened moon (Amavasya) in the shadow without energy and light. The aura of a Siddha Guru who is self-realized is filled with considerable energy and light and radiates this like a full moon to everyone in his/her presence. When seekers make every effort to meditate in the presence of a living Siddha Guru, they are blessed and there is no longer the need of going to pilgrims' places, no need of shastra, no need of mantra, no need of tantra, no need of sadhana (practice). There is even no need of any effort.

A seeker receives everything, by sitting in the presence of a living Siddha Guru. Even if a seeker doesn't feel like meditating, the presence of a living Siddha Guru will draw the seeker into meditation. If the seeker doesn't know how to meditate, just being in the presence of a living Siddha Guru causes the seeker to meditate. That's why having the experience of a living Siddha Guru's presence is very powerful and auspicious.

So choose every opportunity to meditate in the presence of a living Siddha Guru and shine as Parama Atma.

10th Day

Strengthening Inner Soul Energy

Parama Atma is Omnipresent and Omniscient— *a witness to everything*—even while Parama Atma is also equally present in the heart of every human being. The degree of Atma Shakti of every human being is not the same, and spiritual seekers should make the best dedicated efforts to strengthen their inner soul energy (Atma Shakti), just like a person with a strong desire to become wealthy dedicates all his best efforts to earning money and becoming wealthy.

The first and best method to strengthen the inner soul energy (Atma Shakti) is to serve a living Siddha Guru. If the seeker is not blessed with such an opportunity, the second best method is meditation in the presence of a living Siddha Guru. An individual's service to a living Siddha Guru and his/her meditations in the presence of a living Siddha Guru bring dual benefits at the same time—first of wiping out the impurities in the mind and the soul and also greatly strengthening the inner soul energy (Atma Shakti).

If the seeker wants to strengthen the inner soul energy, then he/she has to live in this world untouched, unaffected. The temporal world and Parama Atma are like darkness and Light. If there is Light, then there is no darkness. If there is darkness, then there is no Light. So just like these two, if the seeker has the Darshan of Parama Atma, the world does not exist for him. If the seeker has the darshan of the world, Parama Atma is not possible. The inner soul energy is strengthened with the Darshan of the Parama Atma, and deteriorates with the darshan of the world.

So the spiritual seeker should make very dedicated efforts to meditate in the presence of a living Siddha Guru and attain the Darshan of the Parama Atma. As the mind becomes more and more purified, the strength of the inner soul energy (Atma Shakti) increases. As the individual soul becomes more and more pure, the expansion and strength of the inner soul energy (Atma Shakti) becomes ever more substantial. As the strength of the inner soul energy (Atma Shakti) continues to expand, the seeker will become a great Siddha.

So meditate in the presence of a living Siddha Guru and fully strengthen the inner soul energy

(Atma Shakti) easily and without any effort, and then you will shine as Brahma Gnani—as a great Siddha.

11th Day

Favorite God, Siddha Guru and Parama Shiva

This whole universe with various lokas in it, all beings and things included, is created by Parama Shiva. That is why, every being, every atom in this universe belongs to Parama Shiva. Above all else, seekers should primarily worship Parama Shiva. The surrender of atma and of everything should be done only to Parama Shiva. To attain Parama Shiva, who is formless, is not easy for anyone. That is why every individual must worship and revere these three key things: favorite god, Siddha Guru, and Parama Shiva.

When individuals worship their favorite god and surrender their atma, then the god is pleased by the devotion of the individual and will open up ways for him to meet a Siddha Guru. When the individual worships the Siddha Guru with love and surrenders his atma, the Siddha Guru is pleased and lifts up the individual to Parama Shiva. It is Parama Shiva who gives emancipation (Kaivalyam) by merging the individual into Parama Shiva (this One Life alone).

In this creation, just in the way that every individual has to go forward alone by leaving his father, mother, wife, kids, family members and dear ones, in the end, he also has to leave his favorite god, even his Siddha Guru and has to become one with Parama Shiva and shine as the light. For the seeker to merge with this light is an inevitable law of creation.

So with all your dedicated efforts, surrender your atma to Parama Shiva, and always remember that becoming one with Parama Shiva is your highest and most precious goal. This goal goes beyond your favorite god or Siddha Guru.

Consciously re-direct your love and devotion you have had for your favorite god and Siddha Guru to now allow all this love and devotion to flow into Parama Shiva. Meditate on Parama Shiva and enjoy the infinite bliss with Him. Shiva will be pleased and pour his grace in a continual flow upon you. He will make you one with Him (the One Life alone). He will give you Jivanmukti (emancipation while still here in this world) by making you a Siddha or Avadhuta.

Parama Shiva is the ultimate One and (Nirakara) Shiva is the only one who represents the formless tradition, and (Sakara) Shiva is represented by the eleven (Ekadasa) forms.

On the first day of the deeksha I received a mala and vibhudi from the Nirakara Arunachala Shiva, and on the eleventh day of the deeksha, I received a mala, sandalwood powder, and prasad from Kasi Vishweshwara, one of the eleven forms of Shiva from the Sakara Tattva. Yesterday evening I did my meditation with that mala from Kasi Shiva. Through these two miracle incidents of manifestation by Parama Shiva, it was clearly revealed that Parama Shiva is very pleased with this 18 Day Mouna Dhyana Deeksha.

There was a third miracle from the family's favorite god that revealed how all gods would be pleased if we worship and meditate on Shiva. Our family's god is Urukunda Veeranna swamy. In the month of Sravana (late July through the third week of August), I or one of my family members must visit Veeranna swamy and must worship him and perform abhishekam to him. Because of this deeksha we could not perform this worship or abhishekam. Veeranna swamy was so pleased that he sent me vibhudi and prasadam with love on the 8th day saying, "Your meditations on Shiva are received as the highest of ultimate worship and abhishekam for me." Because of this magical divine incident, it proved to me that this deeksha gave great pleasure to Urukunda Veeranna swamy.

Your meditations and worship of Shiva are an individual's most auspicious practice and will be your protection from misfortunes and setbacks.

12th Day

Mind, the Individual Soul (Jivatma), and Parama Shiva

The Emperor controlling this universe is Parama Shiva, and controlling each body is the individual soul (jivatma). The mind should not give directions to the individual soul; mind should *listen* to its "boss" the individual soul. Then the individual soul will become pure, bright, and can easily merge with Parama Shiva and experience the flow of infinite bliss. If this does not occur and the individual soul listens to the instructions of the mind, the soul becomes contaminated, spiritless, and therefore it will be impossible to merge with Parama Shiva.

When the kama (lust) samskaras, and the moha (delusion) samskaras are very strong inside the mind, then mind does not agree with and will not listen to the words of the individual soul. Because of this, the individual soul becomes like a slave to the mind and listens to its instructions.

For purification: seekers should do meditations intensely and serve a living Siddha Guru, then the samskaras inside the mind diminish, and lose their strength, and the mind will be purified. Because of this, the mind loses its turbulence and becomes quiet. Now this pure and quiet mind agrees with and obeys the instructions from the individual soul.

So the individual soul should always remember it is the "witness" and learn to detach and watch the mind to gain control *over it* by observing. Then the individual soul is released from the grip of maya and becomes one with the Parama Atma.

The individual soul sits in between the mind and the Parama Atma. If the individual soul gets fixated on the mind, or overly attached to the mind, it becomes almost like a slave to it and experiences enormous unhappiness. Otherwise if the individual soul gets attached to and becomes one with Parama Shiva, it attains mukti and will experience infinite bliss.

> The one that does actions is the mind—it is not you the individual soul.

> The one who experiences happiness and unhappiness is the mind—it is not you the individual soul.

The one who experiences gain or loss is the mind—it is not you the individual soul.

The place we experience criticisms and ill fame is in the mind—it is not you the individual soul.

So whatever happens in this world, you should learn to be a witness—to watch the mind as a detached observer without reactions, attachments or aversions—then you will be one with Parama Shiva who is *Sarva Sakshi* and shine as Parama Shiva and rest in infinite bliss.

13th Day

Spiritual Energy (Tapas Shakti)

Meditation blesses you with the *Tapas Shakti* (Spiritual Energy) from Parama Shiva who is Omnipotent—Sarva Sasakudu, commanding beyond all worldly power. People attuned to the world alone have no comprehension of the breadth or depth of this Omnipresent power that commands every heartbeat and breath.

Sacred silence protects the *Tapas Shakti* earned through dedicated meditations without wasting or depleting it. Sacred Silence is incredibly powerful and magnificent just as meditation is marvelous and powerful. That is why Siddha Gurus like Meher Baba, Bhagavan Ramana Maharshi, and Omkarananda Swami stayed in Silence for 40 long years.

When one gives speeches on God, the person receives spiritual merit (punyam), but not the *Tapas Shakti* (spiritual energy). Even though the spiritual merit is received, it diminishes the *Tapas Shakti* (spiritual energy) the person has received through their practice (Upasana). That is why all the Sanatana Maharshis always stayed in

Silence and did meditations, but never gave speeches. They answered disciples' queries, while still avoiding unnecessary speeches.

Those who do meditations with Silence become Siddhas—true Brahma Gnanis. Without meditation, those who use their time listening to speeches or giving speeches, fall into illusions and move away from truth.

Shastras or a Siddha Guru's teachings only give the seeker wisdom, but they cannot immediately purify the mind completely. Therefore the seeker cannot experience the infinite bliss through these teachings alone.

In the same way that external fire burns incense, meditation immediately flames internally to burn the impurities and dissolve darkness [Dosha] inside the mind. This will allow the seeker to experience the flow of infinite bliss. Meditation also burns the bad samskaras, the worst vasanas, to end all the worldly interests of the seeker. It transforms worldly attractions into indifference. It completely dissolves all relationships and attachments in this world.

So, use your precious time for meditations and make the highest use of this lifetime so that your life will be fruitful.

If you meditate properly, you don't need to read any shastras because your loving meditations bless you with knowledge from all the shastras.

If you do your meditations with dedication, you don't need to worship any gods. Meditation blesses you with the benevolence from all gods.

If you do your meditations with great sincerity, you don't need to perform good or pious deeds. Meditation blesses you with the treasure of great spiritual fortune (punya nidhi).

Meditation is the only "way" to clear the mind, to clear the bad qualities, to clear all attachments, to clear the unhappiness, to eliminate all the bad karma (papa nasanam)— to attain the experience of infinite bliss.

So, stop all your words and unnecessary speeches and conversations and do your meditations to have Darshan of Parama Shiva.

14th Day

One Pointed Devotion toward Shiva

The God that was worshipped by the four
Vedas, and the Mother of Vedas ordered
everyone in the universe to worship with one-
pointed devotion—that God is Parama Shiva
alone. Parama Shiva is hiding inside the cave of
every human heart, just like a baby is hidden
inside a mother's womb. Those who rise above
maya and enter into the heart's cave receive the
Darshan of Parama Shiva and Jivanmukti
(emancipation while in the world).

In just the same way that the water in all rivers
originates from the sea and eventually merge
back into the sea, all beings originate from
Parama Shiva and will eventually merge back
into Parama Shiva. This is a rule from the
Supreme Reality. Parama Shiva as the Father for
the whole universe (Sarva Janakudu), is the
supreme ruler and controller (Sarva Niyamitha)
and is the one who witnesses everything (Sarva
Drasta).

So every being must worship, must meditate
upon, must wholeheartedly love only Parama

Shiva. Those who keep Shiva subordinate and worship other gods are like one who holds onto a small piece of discarded glass while ignoring an exquisite diamond. Seekers being deeply involved with worship of a favorite god and Siddha Guru should not forget Shiva. That is why the Mother of Vedas (Veda Mata) opposed the worship of more than one God and established the worship of only the one highest God.

Brahma or Vishnu did not create the whole universe; Sri Rama, Sri Krishnudu, Narasimha Swami did not create it. Neither did Shirdi Sai Baba, Mohammad Pravakta, Jesus, Buddha, or Nanak create it.

As the God above all gods,
Parama Shiva created
the whole universe.

Parama Shiva was famously called by various names like Allah, Father, Lord, Yahweh, Hara, Brahman, Parabrahma.

A seeker will not attain Parama Atma if he/she just explores shastras or religious scriptures without serving a living Siddha Guru or without doing meditations. Only those who thoroughly explore the scripture in their heart (Hrudaya grandham) attain Parama Atma.

If the seekers just study shastras or religious scriptures without turning the mind inward through meditations, they might become learned persons on the subject they studied; but they will never attain Parama Atma. They might get information about illusions, false knowledge, but not the true knowledge of Brahman.

So with service to a living Siddha Guru and uninterrupted devotion to meditations—a seeker will experience the inner Soul. Just as the sun shines brightly when the clouds move away; through meditation the darkness of maya is dissolved, and Shiva gives Darshan with the brilliance of crore (1,000,000) suns together. Therefore with all your heart, do meditations with determination, consistency, and intensity and shine forth as Shiva.

15th Day

Meditating in the Presence of a Living Siddha Guru

In this Kali Yuga the easiest and most *expedient* method for all human beings to advance is to meditate in the presence of a living Siddha Guru. For those who are not yet blessed with the opportunity to serve a living Siddha Guru they should at the very least, meditate in the presence of a living Siddha Guru. Such meditations will be enough; they will make the seeker a Brahma Gnani.

Meditations done in the presence of a living Siddha Guru are much different than meditations done with only a seeker's own effort. Even Devatas can't completely describe the great benefit and effect of being in the presence of a living Siddha Guru. The spiritual attunement and vibrations of such a Guru are many, many times higher than the Masters who have attained mahasamadhi. The reason for this magnitude is that kundalini Shakti (power) is over-flowing as streams of infinite bliss and divine energy.

In the same way that pitch darkness disappears completely when the sun rises in the morning; the seekers' darkness of illusion disappears completely when they enter into the presence of a living Siddha Guru.

And just as the world brightens up when the sun rises, the seekers are filled with "divine brightness" when they close their eyes while in the presence of a living Siddha Guru.

Just as the whole world quiets down when the moon comes up, a seeker's mind quiets down to be filled with infinite bliss when they meditate in the presence of a living Siddha Guru.

A Siddha Guru's Atma Shakti is inherently present and infused in his every exhale of breath, and seekers receive the Atma Shakti within a few moments of being exposed to the exhales of a living Siddha Guru. A seeker's individual soul is energized and brightens up because of this.

A Siddha Guru's Yoga Shakti is also hidden in his every exhale. When a Siddha Guru exhales, seekers receive this Yoga Shakti. Thus the strength of a seeker's Atma increases, resulting in significant positive impacts—diseases are cured and chakras are cleansed.

Infinite Prana Shakti is inherently present in every exhale (niswasa) of a Siddha Guru and seekers receive this Prana Shakti when they are exposed to his exhale. With this exposure, the mind becomes very quiet and seekers will experience the bliss of soul (Atmanadam).

When a Siddha Guru closes his eyes, a stream of energy comes out from the Siddha Guru's 7 chakras, and surrounds all sides of the subtle body of the seeker. Because of this, a seeker's mind, intellect (buddi) and individual soul (jivatma) are purified, and the Subtle body (Linga Sarira) becomes very energized.

A seeker meditating with his own effort compares to spending time to take care of a crop, harvesting it with tons and tons of hard work, and then preparing it as a meal. While a seeker meditating in the presence of a living Siddha Guru compares to eating a meal that has been already prepared and served on the plate ready to eat.

A seeker meditating only with his own effort is like saving money by adding one penny at a time, while a seeker meditating in the presence of a living Siddha Guru is like receiving a gift of one crore rupees without any effort.

So meditate in the presence of a living Siddha Guru and become a Brahma Gnani.

16th Day

Sleep, Nirvikalpa Samadhi

Parama Atma provided *Nirvikalpa Samadhi* (alert stillness) and sleep to bless all human beings, just as he created day and night as a blessing for all creatures. Nirvikalpa Samadhi is like the day while sleep is like the night.

In Nirvikalpa Samadhi one is filled with cosmic consciousness and is consciously aware of eternal knowledge and infinite bliss; in contrast, sleep renders one unconscious and unaware in a subconscious and illusory reality. In sleep one finds only an impure dullness as a flawed reflection of maya. Though all creatures go through the experience of sleep, only one in millions of human beings will attain the Nirvikalpa Samadhi, the highest awareness. The reason that so few attain is because Nirvikalpa Samadhi is a pure egoless reflection of Parama Shiva.

Just to get into a sleep state one does not need any kind of practice, but more intense practice (sadhana) is essential to reach Nirvikalpa

Samadhi which requires that a seeker meditate in the presence of a living Siddha Guru.

Just as an extremely tired person can quickly go into deep sleep without much effort, a seeker should be able to go easily into samadhi without any effort. Like a person yearns for sleep after being awake for 24 hours, a seeker yearns with increased longings to enter the samadhi state. An overly tired person easily becomes still in a deep sleep, and likewise, a seeker should be able to experience the deep stillness of samadhi for at least a few hours. To be blessed with attaining this extended deep stillness a seeker should serve a living Siddha Guru and do intense meditations.

When the seeker reaches a state where he/she can stay in the Nirvikalpa Samadhi for even a few moments, all the samskaras in the seeker's mind begin to fade out—any strong weakness for lust, attachments, aversions, and bad qualities that cloud the seeker's mind, are purged and eliminated; therefore the ego is completely wiped out to allow pure reflection.

One can't become Brahma Gnani, just by reading 100 shastras or even millions of shastras. The pious one that is established in the Nirvikalpa Samadhi, even for one moment, is a true Brahma Gnani. To get into this wonderful pure state you should do Dhyana Tapasu with dedication and determination.

An onion contains many skins and when one layer is removed another one becomes visible. Similarly there are many layers of weakness of the soul. These weaknesses are dissolved one by one while the seeker is meditating in the presence of a living Siddha Guru. The seeker will be blessed with the experience of Nirvikalpa Samadhi when all the weaknesses of the soul are completely dissolved. Whenever the dedicated seeker wants to have the Darshan of the Parama Shiva, it surely can be theirs.

Seekers who are doing extensive meditations should never be disappointed and think, "I have not gotten into the samadhi state." They should always remember that with each of their dedicated meditations even more of the weaknesses of the soul are being dissolved. So with great patience and LOVE, serve a living Siddha Guru and do intensive meditations to attain Jivanmukti and become a Siddha.

17th Day

Inner Silence (Mano Mounam)

Parama Shiva who is the supreme or transcendent place (Parama Dhaam) and the ultimate "Father" (Parama Pita) —is far above talk (vak), mind, and emotions (bhava). Only seekers who do their meditations in silence will get the Darshan of Parama Shiva. Those who talk, those who think too much, and those who are full of many emotions, will not get the Darshan of Parama Shiva even in millions (crores) of lifetimes; they won't experience the flow of infinite bliss.

> This wonderful opportunity
> is attained only through
> complete silence.

There are two types of silence: The first one is an outer silence (vak mounam) and the second one is an inner silence (mano mounam). Outer silence (vak mounam) is similar to being a mute person who has no voice. Inner silence (mano mounam) is when the mind has merged with Parama Atma and remains in the ocean of infinite bliss. Everyone can establish themselves in the state of outer silence, but very few are adequately prepared to establish themselves in the inner silence.

It is much easier to control the mouth and keep from speaking, but much, much harder to control the mind to keep from thinking. Similar to the way a fish suffers and struggles vigorously when it is out of water, the mind suffers and struggles to remain still. The suffering and turbulent mind, devoid of peace, threatens and scares the individual soul (jivatma) and continuously causes itself considerable unhappiness. A constantly busy mind makes it very tough for the seeker to practice stillness and to be established in the inner-silence state. That is why when ten million (crore) people meditate, there may be only one of them who will succeed to be established in a state of inner silence.

To make progress and be established in an inner-silence state a seeker must practice in three ways:

1. in maintaining outer silence,
2. in service to the living Siddha Guru,
3. in intense meditations (Dhyana Tapasu).

With the practice of outer silence the mind becomes more and more aloof from worldly attachments and happiness from worldly things. Mind no longer has a turbulent nature and dwells in a calm state. Through its service to the living Siddha Guru, the mind is continually purified and energized; bad qualities and deceptions (moha samskaras)* become extremely weak and completely fade away. Mind is thus prepared, ready, and eager to enjoy the flow of infinite bliss; because of this, mind now has great interest and intense longing to do meditations. As soon as the seeker enters into the meditative state, the mind starts hurrying toward Parama Shiva, and with little effort it merges with Parama Shiva. This is the great secret of how to prepare one's self to achieve a merger of the mind (mano layam) with Parama Shiva. Only continuing in these three practices will achieve the Darshan of Parama Shiva.

Until the mind is quiet, Parama Atma is concealed and infinite bliss won't flow in the inner space. The seeker is able to see the Parama Shiva very clearly only at the moment the seeker is established in inner silence. When the individual soul merges with Parama Shiva, it shines as the ultimate light (Parama Jyoti), as the ultimate knowledge——while streams of infinite bliss flow in the inner space.

Until the mind is quiet, a seeker can't hear the divine guidance from Parama Atma; however, a seeker will hear the divine voice once he/she is established in the inner silence. The divine voice cannot be heard through the physical ears or through the mind. The divine voice is the primal sound—the first sound, far above and beyond any worldly sound. So as long as you talk, you can't hear the voice from the ultimate God.

If you want to hear the voice from the ultimate God, you must become silent and do intense meditations. So as much as possible:

> Practice inner silence,
> Do intense meditations,
> Serve a living Siddha Guru,

in order to make the best use of this life and achieve the ultimate goal (kaivalyam).

*Moha samskaras: deceptive impressions in the mind related to delusion or infatuations.

18th Day

The Only Real Path to Attain
the Darshan of Parama Atma

Even though there are many spiritual paths, traditions and religions, if we question, "Whose darshan should human beings get, or what should human beings attain?", the one and only answer we receive for these questions from all religions, all spiritual paths, all Vedas is: "attain the Darshan of Parama Shiva and enjoy the infinite bliss."

Some say, to attain the Darshan of Parama Atma there are many paths, but this is not truth. That is only an erroneous belief or illusion of learned kavis, pandits, and ordinary gurus.

Those who understand the inner meanings of Sanatana Maharshis, those who understand the heart of the Veda Mata—those who hear the inner sound and guidance in their meditations—only these people understand that there are no multiple paths to attain the Darshan of Parama Atma; there is one and only one path, which is meditation on Shiva in the presence of a living

Siddha Guru. This is the path; this is the target; this is the goal.

But some may question: "There are many paths such as, the path of devotion, the path of knowledge (Jnana), the path of yoga, and the path of divine love. What is the target with these paths? If these are not the real path, why are many human beings following them?

These various paths can only take seekers to a junction or center point; but none of these will take anyone to the Darshan of Parama Atma. Meditation is the only path that takes seekers from this center point to the Darshan of Parama Atma. Paths like devotion, knowledge, love, or using mantras only take the seeker to this junction point, which is the goal for these paths.

There are also differences between these paths. For example, the path of devotion is higher than the path of karma. The path of knowledge is higher than the path of devotion, the path of yoga is higher than the path of knowledge, the path of love is higher than the path of yoga, the path of meditation is higher than the path of love...A seeker may encounter can experience many difficulties if he or she does not understand these differences. For instance, a seeker who doesn't understand the truth, won't experience infinite bliss, and therefore, won't get the Darshan of Parama Atma.

The one and only path in this Kaliyuga is "meditation on Shiva with the service to a living Siddha Guru." A meditation on Shiva is a meditation of formlessness; this is a meditation on incorporeality, the highest Divinity.

About the Author

Siddha Guru Ramanananda Maharshi came to this world on April 27, 1967 in the village of Kapatrala India; he was named Venkata Ramanaiah Guduru, as the 16th and last child born to Narasaiah and Nagamma Guduru. At the early age of 5 his parents noted his exceptional spiritual inclination when he devoted a few hours each day worshipping idols in his home. Every day after school he brought flowers, turmeric and kumkam to Para Shakthi Temple to worship the idol.

When he was in the 4th grade, his family moved from Kapatrala village to Kurnool. Here he loved to sing bhajans. Within a short period his voice became very melodious and he continued to develop this musical worship for about 8 years. When Maharshi was in the 9th grade his mother passed away, and during this time he did not cease from his daily ritual to Adi Para Shakthi to obey the death traditions of stopping external rituals to the idols. Instead, Maharshi followed his heart and continued with his usual daily rituals and devotions.

In his second year as an undergraduate in Mechanical Engineering at JNTU, Ananthapoor, the inquiry of tattva started within him. Whenever he opened an academic book to read, immediately, he would hear an inner voice from his heart say, "*Fool, were you born to read these academic books?"* making it very difficult to focus on his academics. Often his inner voice would ask, *"What is the real purpose of this life?"*

Looking at the hills and mountains, questions came, *"Who placed this big hill here?" "How did this come here?"* Similarly, one day while looking at the Sun, he thought, *"Without any support, how is the sun in the sky?"* Pressure to study for exams, distracted him from going deeply into these inquiries. His external ritual to Para Shakthi was stopped and instead of singing devotional songs, he sang songs from movies and his four undergraduate years were spent focusing on both academics and inner inquiry about the real purpose of life.

Chanting of "Om Namo Bhagavathe Vasudevaya"

After completing his undergraduate engineering degree in 1991, Maharshi moved to Vizag for his Masters program. In 1993 he attended a discourse on Bhagavatham by a swamij and learned about Narada's instructing Prahlada to chant "Om Namo Bhagavathe Vasudevaya." These words made Maharshi feel happy, and without enquiring into the meaning of the chant he started chanting it, but after a time Maharshi suspected chanting the mantra might be causing the difficulties he was experiencing. When living expenses had used all his money he moved to Hyderabad in search of a job and accepted a position as an engineer in a factory. On the second day at work, he once again began to hear an inner voice, *"Fool, were you born to do the works like these?"* There seemed to be no other way to support himself. After working for two months, he rejected this repetitious and monotonous life of getting up early in the morning, going to work, coming home late in the night, sleeping, and then repeating the same routine each day.

He soon quit the engineering job and became a math teacher, while continuing his music classes. Maharshi realized that the chanting of the mantra must be the root-cause for his conflicts and he asked a yogi to explain it. The yogi replied, "You have asked God of devotion for gnana (knowledge), aversion, penance, and now Vasudeva has given them to you. That is why these difficulties have come because this is a mantra of liberation, and a most powerful one.

Inner Chanting of "Om Namah Shivaya" by Lord Venkateswara

Maharshi visited Tirupati in January 1994. He heard the chant of **"Om Namah Shivaya"** when entering into the inner sanctum for the darshan of Lord Venkateswara and was immediately enveloped with immense happiness in that very moment. He recognized this as instruction from the Lord and started chanting the mantra. Maharshi observed that difficulties began to fade with the chanting of this mantra, to reveal peace and happiness within him. He was also having darshan of Shiva Linga daily and began questioning what difference was there between the outer Shiva Linga and the inner Shiva Spiritual Presence.

Darshan of Ramakrishna Paramahamsa, and Swami Vivekananda

Maharshi visited Ramakrishna Paramahamsa Ashramam in March of 1994. When he went to the Ashramam bookstore he did not have money for a book but he read a sign there, "Kamini – Kanchanale Maya (Woman and Money are real Maya)." Standing in front of Ramakrishna Paramahamsa's statue he heartfully asked, "Swamy, you say, "Woman and Money are real Maya, but I need money to get a book of your teachings. Can you give this to me for free?" Asking this sincerely, Maharshi returned home.

To his surprise, a gentleman of slight acquaintance came to his home with a bundle of books and asked Maharshi to keep the books until he would pick them up at a later date. In the bundle were 5 books of Ramakrishna Paramahamsa's and 10 books of Swami Vivekananda's. Maharshi was astonished at how the books had come to him without money. After this incident he felt a very keen interest to read more spiritual books and he studied all the books he could get with great reverence.

In 1997 Maharshi had the vision of Vivekananda Swami with a divine glow, wearing a saffron dress and speaking a few words in a divine flow. Swami then departed in a divine airplane after looking at Maharshi very seriously. The very next day, Ramakrishna Paramahamsa gave a darshan; with his hand on his chin, he said smiling, "You sing very well," and Maharshi was enveloped in a divine glow beyond any words to describe it.

Divine Manifestation of Parama Guru – Shirdi Sai Baba

Maharshi did not know nor hear about Baba before 1994, or even know there were already many books telling of his life's history. Maharshi did not participate in his bhajans and also did not visit his temple.

Because there was a Sai Baba Temple in Kurnool, Maharshi at first thought Sai Baba was also a god just like Sri Rama and Sri Krishna, and that he also belonged to the age of Puranas. He did not know that Sai Baba lived like an ordinary common man, and that there were many Sai devotees and followers just as it was with Sri Rama, Sri Krishna, and Shiva.

Baba's words: *"I bring them to me whoever belongs to me. There is no difference between myself and my photo."* Maharshi himself says— These words have literally come true in my own life. Some become devotees of Baba after getting the vision of Baba in their dreams; some after studying his books and hearing of his miracles; some after watching miracles happen to their neighbors; still others through participation in bhajans and satsangs. But for myself, I fell in Love with Baba when seeing him through his photo for the first time.

First Darshan of Baba's Photo – Effect

In the month of April 1994, Maharshi went to buy pictures of gods to place in his room. As he was leaving the shop, a person at a distance approached him saying, "This is Shirdi Sai Baba's original photo; buy this also," then he placed Baba's picture in Maharshi's hands. When he heard Baba's name for the first time and looked at the photo, he immediately felt a shock-like current flow through him. For a few moments his mind was stilled and then he happily bought the photo. With the first darshan of Shirdi Sai, Maharshi's mind became so very quiet and peaceful that he forgot his sense of the body. Later Maharshi came to understand these experiences after reading Baba's life history that tells how many other devotees first came to him in similar ways.

Divine Manifestation of Baba – Second Time

After buying the picture, Maharshi went to his friend Rajasekhar's house upon an invitation for dinner and he slept over. That night he had a dream where suddenly the room was filled with light from which Baba's form emerged. Baba's face was glowing very brightly as he came and touched Maharshi's head with his little finger; immediately the two flew to the sky and Baba then disappeared. This dream was very clear and when Maharshi awoke he was filled with great tranquility, happiness and peace—and later even after awaking, Baba's form remained standing in his heart.

His dream urged Maharshi to read the life history of Shirdi Sai to learn more about Baba. As soon as he finished Baba's book he wanted to visit the town of Shirdi but he could not go because just then he got news that his father had passed away. Maharshi wondered why such an unpleasant thing happened after reading Baba's book. He started to question, "Is this devotion a waste of time?"

On his way to his home town, Maharshi opened a book of Baba's and saw these words in it, *"You will receive my grace from your house."* Then he had some angry thoughts, "Baba's grace should bring pleasant things, why are these unpleasant things now happening? What is your grace? This is all hallucinations of the mind."

As soon as Maharshi reached his family's home, his brother offered him Baba's prasad, vibhudhi, an audio cassette, and a picture of Baba. While applying vibhudi on his forehead, Maharshi remembered Baba's words, *"You will get my grace from your house."* From this point on Maharshi made a serious personal commitment never to lose faith in Baba—even for a second. He also found numerous spiritual books in his father's room and while reading through all the books, he realized that his father was also a great spiritual seeker.

The First Visit to Shirdi

In 1994 when Maharshi visited Shirdi for the first time during Navratri on Ashtami day, tears rolled down his cheeks and unknown memories flooded his mind when he entered into Dwarakamai. In Samadhi Mandir, he heard, "Om Namah Shivaya" just like he had heard it in the Tirupati Balaji Temple. When Maharshi experienced divine bliss in Shirdi, he forgot about whatever was happening around him and whether he had money for his travels, etc. He was consumed with the longing for self-realization and longed for the support of a living guru.

When he wanted to focus on his spiritual life, he realized that his life was already in Baba's hands. In March of 1995 Maharshi was married to Vijaya Lakshmi, and they now have two lovely daughters, Bhavani and Shivani. Even following marriage his focus continues to be primarily on his spiritual life, intensely requesting Baba's grace.

On June 29, 1995 through the grace of Shirdi Sai Baba, Ramanananda Maharshi attained darshan of Parama Atma and experienced Nirvikalpa Samadhi continuing for 21 days. While Maharshi had not done tremendous spiritual practice previous to attaining the state of samadhi, he had had a very intense longing for it in his heart. Maharshi believes that it was the longing of his heart which led him to Guru Shirdi Sai.

After self-realization, he wanted to stay in samadhi, but his Guru Shirdi Sai had different plans for Maharshi. Under the guidance of Shirdi Sai, Maharshi wrote his first book called "*Atma Darshana Anubhuti*." As research on Shirdi Sai, he interviewed descendants (sons, grandsons etc.) of 27 direct disciples of Shirdi Sai to produce several volumes. One of these was *Paramaguruvutho Sahajeevanam* (Living with Paramaguru), and his other books *Atmadarshana Anubhuti, Shaktipaatam, Shirdi Sai Anugraha Rahasyam*, and *Shirdi Sai Seva Rahasyam* are great storehouses of power and knowledge.

As seekers read his books, these powerful teachings that are simply and clearly presented will open the way to further advances in spiritual progress. From his deep divine love for Shirdi Sai, Maharshi has also composed several songs and released many superb music albums.

In 2012, Maharshi began introducing Shiva to his disciples, sharing numerous outstanding discourses on Shiva, including Shirdi Sai as well. Through the immense grace of Param Guru Shirdi Sai, Maharshi is blessed with a unique ability to transmit divine teachings to others (Shaktipaata Siddhi).

Maharshi now resides in Hyderabad, India, where he conducts regular meditation sessions for spiritual seekers through Shaktipaatham. During these very powerful meditations with Maharshi, many participants are inspired with divine visions; they experience encouragement and healings of health problems with an increasing joy for life. Many seekers advance to find their inner heart opens to take them much closer to the darshan of Parama Shiva.

In 2014, a huge piece of land on the outskirts of greater Hyderabad was selected by Maharshi for a future Ashramam. He named this place "Shiva Shakthi Shirdi Sai Anugraha Maha Peetam" — also calling it "Ramaneswaram." This new Ashramam can accommodate a large number of people. Thousands may gather to attend various special events conducted for devotees such as during Shivaratri and special meditation activities.